THE DIGITAL ADVERTISING GUIDE

THE COMPLETE GUIDE FOR TODAY'S DIGITAL MARKETER

First Printing: February 2014.

ISBN 978-0-578-13822-0

Overdrive Marketing Communications, LLC
38 Everett Street, Suite 201
Allston, MA 02134
USA

http://www.ovrdrv.com
http://www.ovrdrv.com/blog
http://www.facebook.com/overdriveinteractive
http://www.twitter.com/ovrdrv
http://plus.google.com/+ovrdrv
http://www.linkedin.com/company/overdrive-interactive

TABLE OF CONTENTS

INTRODUCTION

Ok, so why did we create The Digital Advertising Guide? Because the reality of today's digital advertising is that it's not digital advertising! It's just advertising. No matter who you are, what your title is or what you are selling, you need to understand digital. Why? Because nearly every campaign has online components and destinations.

So what does that mean for all of us who work in advertising and marketing? It means we all have to be digital marketers in order to be great marketers. We all have to have our heads around the terms, technologies and concepts of the online marketing world. Does this mean you have to be a digital designer, developer or engineer? No! But it does mean you have to be conversant in digital media and marketing and speak with digital designers, developers and engineers. You have to understand what is possible and how to articulate what you want done. And after that, you need to know how to measure success.

So that's why we wrote The Digital Advertising Guide. We wrote it to help everyone become not just better online marketers, but better marketers!

Enjoy!

Harry J. Gold
CEO, Overdrive Interactive

DESKTOP / LAPTOP DISPLAY

OVERVIEW

Within the industry, "Display" typically means banner advertising or other forms of graphical imagery and text used to advertise on a webpage. Display comes in a variety of sizes and formats, with different methods for purchasing, serving, and reporting. It is a complex and ever-changing medium, which makes it challenging to keep up with the constant innovation and the universe of options.

Below are examples of the most commonly purchased Display ad units according to the Interactive Advertising Bureau (IAB). These sizes may be found on desktop, laptop or tablet devices.

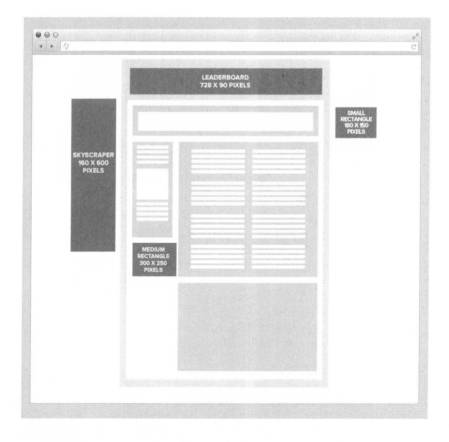

S I Z E S

STANDARD IAB SIZES

Standard banner sizes were defined by the Internet Advertising Bureau (IAB) to enable marketers to simultaneously work with multiple media partners. With standardized size requirements, advertisers are able to produce one set of banners for all their media partners. Standardization also enables ad networks to serve banners across many websites, since the vast majority of websites voluntarily adhere to these IAB sizes. You can learn more about the IAB at IAB. net.

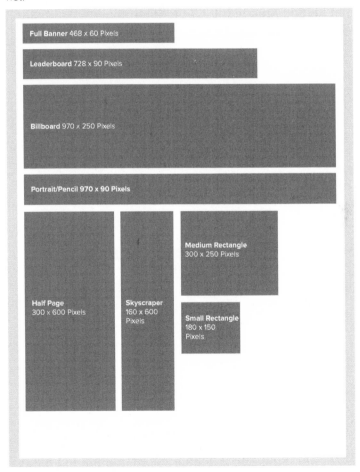

The above banners are the most commonly produced and distributed sizes.
Visit http://www.iab.net for more information.

EXPANDABLE BANNERS

There are a few expandable banners which the IAB calls "rising stars." These provide a more significant presence on a website than standard banners.

Pushdown

A pushdown is an expandable banner located at the top of a webpage that expands downward, covering some of the content of the page, when rolled over or clicked.

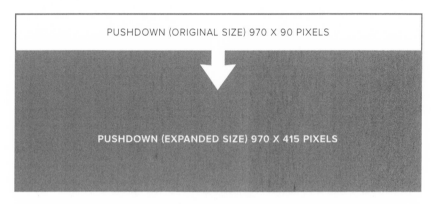

PUSHDOWN (ORIGINAL SIZE) 970 X 90 PIXELS

PUSHDOWN (EXPANDED SIZE) 970 X 415 PIXELS

When a person first sees the pushdown, it is a small banner—970 x 90 pixels—located at the top of a webpage.

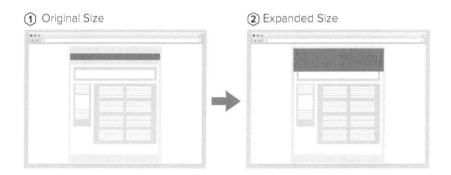

① Original Size   ② Expanded Size

Once someone clicks or rolls over it, the pushdown extends down over some of the content of a page becoming a 970 x 415 pixel banner.

Slider

A slider is an expandable banner located at the bottom of a webpage that expands upward, covering some of the content of the page, when rolled over or clicked.

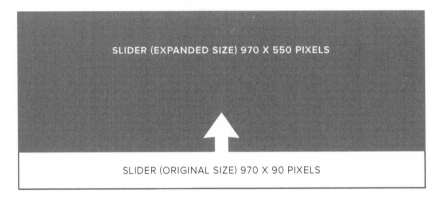

SLIDER (EXPANDED SIZE) 970 X 550 PIXELS

SLIDER (ORIGINAL SIZE) 970 X 90 PIXELS

When a person first sees the slider, it is a small banner—only 950 x 90 pixels—located at the bottom of a webpage.

① Original Size   ② Expanded Size

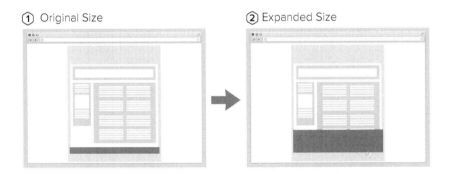

Once someone clicks or rolls over it, the slider then extends up over some of the content of a page, becoming a 950 x 550 pixel banner.

Sidekick

A sidekick is a medium-size rectangular banner that expands out from the right side of a webpage, covering some of the content of the page, when rolled over or clicked.

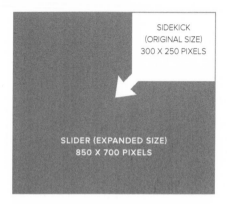

SIDEKICK
(ORIGINAL SIZE)
300 X 250 PIXELS

SLIDER (EXPANDED SIZE)
850 X 700 PIXELS

When a person first sees the sidekick banner, it looks like a standard 300 x 250 pixel ad unit.

① Original Size   ② Expanded Size

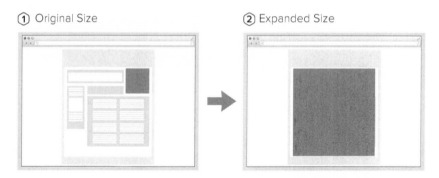

However, once someone clicks or rolls over the banner, it extends diagonally out over the content of a page, becoming a 850 x 700 pixel banner.

NON-STANDARD AD UNITS

While the IAB has defined many common banner sizes, there are other options that have yet to be strictly defined. The following ad units are also popular, but because websites set requirements individually, sizes and specifications may vary between sites. These units are typically purchased directly from publishers by advertisers, rather than through ad networks.

Skins

Skins, also known as wallpapers, are customizable and interchangeable background graphics for a webpage or a desktop. Skins may be clickable and can direct users to an external site.

① Without Skin   ② With Skin

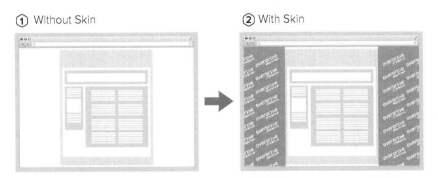

In this example, the unused sides of a webpage are tiled or patterned with a brand's logo.

Rails

Rails are wide skyscraper-style ads that line both the right and left side of a webpage, but not the entire background. Rails may be clickable and can direct users to an external site.

① Without Rails   ② With Rails

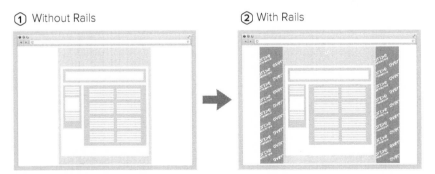

Like with a skin, the unused sides of a webpage are filled with long and narrow banners.

Page Overlays

Page overlays are ad units that appear over the content of a webpage, rendering the rest of the page inactive until the ad is closed. If a viewer chooses to close the page overlay, the original webpage becomes accessible. There is always a "Close" or "X" button, usually in one of the corners, that lets users opt to not engage with the ad. Typically these ads are served when a webpage is accessed from an external link. Page overlays should not to be confused with pop-up or pop-under ads.

① Without Page Overlay   ② With Page Overlay

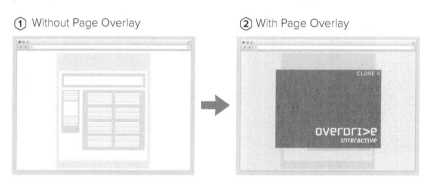

In this example, the page overlay ad appears over the original content of the webpage, within the same web browser window. The webpage behind the page overlay is greyed out, rendering its content inactive.

Pop-ups

Pop-ups are ad units that open in a new web browser window, in front of the window being viewed. Pop-ups are often considered impolite, as they are more invasive than other display ad units. In fact, many browsers and applications have developed plug-ins to automatically block these ads from serving.

① Without Pop-up   ② With Pop-up

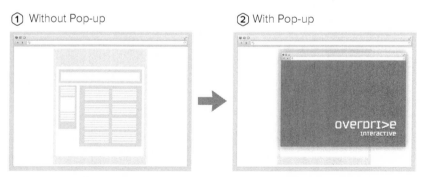

In this example, a pop-up ad has opened in a new web browser window, in front of the webpage being viewed.

Pop-unders

Pop-unders are ad units that open in a new web browser window, behind the
window being viewed. Pop-unders are
also considered impolite.

① Without Pop-under   ② With Pop-under

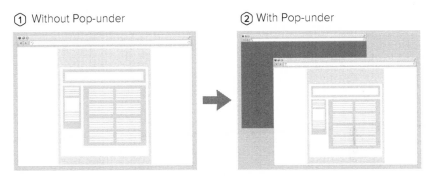

In this example, a pop-under ad has opened in a new web browser window,
behind the webpage being viewed. When the window is closed, the user will see
the pop-under.

Interstitials

An interstitial is a large-format ad unit, typically the size of a whole webpage, that is displayed before a user can see a website's content, or when navigating from one page to another within the same website. It essentially functions as a webpage that a user must view before arriving at the destination page.

 Newsletter with link

In this example, an individual clicks a text link in an email newsletter to read an article. (Users may also click to a destination website from another site or directly type in a URL.)

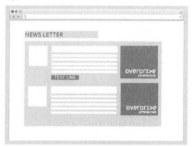 Interstitial Ad

Before the user reaches the webpage, the interstitial is served as a unique page. The user may choose to either click the ad, view the ad in its entirety, or skip the interstitial by clicking the "Close" or "Skip" button, which is usually located on one of the ad's corners.

 Destination Page

Once the interstitial ad's animation has ended or the ad has been closed, the user will be redirected to the URL

Peelbacks

A peelback is an ad unit that unveils itself across the content of a webpage when clicked on or rolled over, as if the click was turning a page in a book.

(1) Original Size

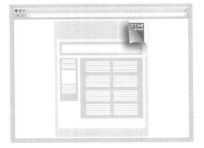

(2) Expanded Size

In this example, the user is teased with a small portion of the peelback's copy and imagery on the upper right-hand corner of the webpage. Often, the teaser moves slightly to entice viewers to click or roll over it. When the user does click or roll over the teaser, the webpage content peels back, revealing a larger view of the ad behind it.

AD FORMATS

The format of an ad is dictated by the specifications of the website on which it will run and by the purpose of the marketing. The most common formats include standard, Flash animation, and rich media.

STANDARD BANNERS

Standard banners consist of any combination of static or animated imagery and text in a .jpg, .gif, or .png file. This is the most basic format and the one with the lowest file size.

Standard banners click through to a single destination URL and do not offer any other type of viewer interaction. They also serve as a backup banner in case a Flash or a rich-media banner cannot be served. This may occur when the page is viewed on a browser or device that does not support Flash, as is the case with certain tablets, including the iPad and Kindle.

Static banners are the simplest forms of banners. These single-frame gifs or jpegs do not have any moving images.

Animated GIF or JPEG Banners

Animated gifs contain multiple frames, or rotations, which create an animation effect. They are looped automatically and typically up to three times.

① First Frame   ② Second Frame   ③ Third Frame

(With three loops)

FLASH BANNERS

Flash animation banners are a combination of animated imagery and text that are created with Adobe Flash. Flash banners are more dynamic and exciting than standard banners. The banners display a series of messages and images, and thus provide more real estate for content. Currently, Flash banners cannot run on an iPad and some other tablet devices, so animated gifs may still be required.

In the example above, the original standard banner was re-done using Flash to connect different parts of the content.

RICH MEDIA BANNERS

Rich-media banners provide the most viewer interaction and engagement features. The banners encourage clicks, roll overs, transactions, and other measurable online actions. Due to their complexity, there are higher ad serving and development costs associated with rich-media banners. The next section will explore rich media banners in more detail.

RICH MEDIA

While most banner advertising drives users to a landing page to complete an action or generate a conversion, rich-media banners engage users even if they don't click through to a separate website. The capabilities of a rich-media ad include, but are not limited to:

+ Capturing data
+ Sending Calendar reminders
+ Expanding
+ Delivering coupons
+ Delivering special offers
+ Feeding in data-driven content
+ Housing a game
+ Housing a survey or poll
+ Sending Instant messages or emails
+ Offering content (such as whitepapers, case studies, etc.) for download
+ Playing a music clip
+ Playing a video
+ Providing e-commerce capabilities
+ Sending an e-card or postcard
+ Showing a gallery of images
+ Showing a live feed
+ Showing movie times
+ Showing nearest retail locations
+ Showing weather forecasts
+ Social sharing
+ Widget sharing
+ Other interactive elements

SAMPLE RICH MEDIA: VIDEOS AND LEAD CAPTURE

① Original Size

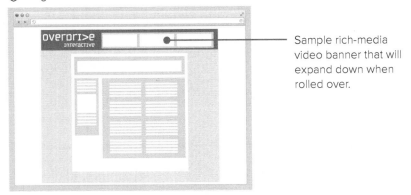

Sample rich-media video banner that will expand down when rolled over.

② Expanded Size

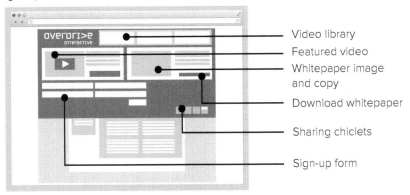

Video library

Featured video

Whitepaper image and copy

Download whitepaper

Sharing chiclets

Sign-up form

In this example, the rich-media banner initially appears as a standard leaderboard with a selection of videos. Once a user rolls over or clicks on the rich-media banner, it expands downward over the content of a webpage into a larger banner. The expanded banner now accommodates more content and interactive features, such as a video library and featured videos, an optional white paper download, social sharing chiclets, and a lead-capture form.

SAMPLE RICH MEDIA: FUN GAME

① Original Size

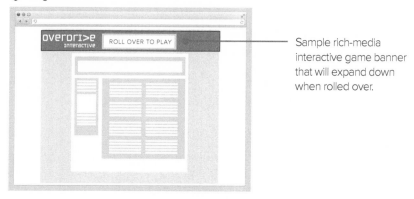

Sample rich-media interactive game banner that will expand down when rolled over.

② Expanded Size

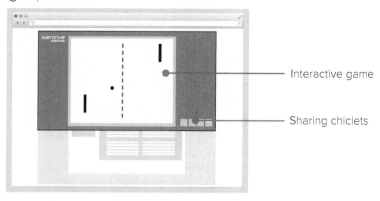

Interactive game

Sharing chiclets

In this example, the rich-media banner also starts as a standard leaderboard. It then expands downward, over the content of the webpage, to accommodate a game and social sharing chiclets.

RICH-MEDIA VENDORS

There are several vendors that specialize in providing rich media serving and development tools for marketers to create rich-media banners. Popular vendors include:

CONVERSANT	www.conversantmedia.com
FLASHTALKING	www.flashtalking.com
POINTROLL	www.pointroll.com
MEDIAMIND	www.mediamind.com
DOUBLECLICK	www.google.com/doubleclick
MEDIALETS	www.medialets.com
INTERPOLLS	www.interpolls.com
PICTELA	www.pictela.com
LINKSTORM	www.linkstorms.com

MEASUREMENT & TRACKING

While standard and Flash banners are able to record delivered impressions and banner clicks, the advanced coding
required to build rich-media banners also allows for advanced performance tracking.

Specific rich-media engagement metrics include, but are not limited to:

+ Time spent with the banner

+ Which parts of the banner were most focused on

+ Number of conversions

+ Number of closes or exits

+ Number of downloads

+ Number of leads captured

+ Number of shares

+ Video/play metrics

+ Survey/polling results

BUYING METHODS

Display is typically purchased through three types of media-distribution vendors: publisher direct, ad networks, and ad exchanges.

PUBLISHER DIRECT

A publisher is an individual website or organization that manages and disseminates content for public distribution or sale. Buying inventory directly from publishers allows marketers to negotiate and purchase more premium media real estate, including content-integration opportunities, sponsorships, and other unique offerings. Publishers include websites that focus on specific information such as news, entertainment, or sports.

Sample Publishers

Selecting the appropriate publisher for a campaign will depend on the target audience. For example, marketers interested in reaching women between the ages of 25 and 34 may consider publishers such as:

+ iVillage

+ Daily Candy

+ People

+ Vogue

+ Martha Stewart

+ Sheknows

+ Glamour

+ Women's Health

+ Oprah.com

+ Shape

+ Real Simple

+ Self

Purchasing Publisher Direct Content

Media buyers contact the publishers' sales departments to get proposals and secure ad inventory.

AD NETWORKS

An ad network is an aggregator or broker of advertising inventory for many publishers. Buying inventory from ad networks allows marketers to buy ad space from multiple publishers through a single partner. This method allows for extended reach and lower pricing.

While there are general ad networks that aggregate and broker a variety of publishers, there are also more specialized
networks that are specifically tailored to suit various marketing needs. Some of the more specialized networks include:

Vertical

A vertical ad network sells inventory from many sites that fall under a single content umbrella. For example, an ad network may specialize in the information technology (IT) vertical.

Premium

A premium ad network sells inventory only from comScore's list of the top 100 media properties, which have been categorized as the most trafficked and well-known sites across the Internet.

Long-tail

A long-tail ad network sells inventory from comScore's extended list of media properties, which have been categorized as sites that are much smaller and less well-known across the Internet.

Local

A local ad network sells inventory from regional or geographically targeted sites.

Affiliate

An affiliate ad network sells inventory from sites that use a cost-per-action revenue-share model between the advertisers, the publishers, and the network.

Blind

A blind ad network does not share the list of publishers that it purchases inventory from, but may sometimes give examples of publishers.

Transparent

A transparent ad network shares the full list of publishers that it purchases inventory from, and will sometimes let marketers pick and choose which ones they wish to include in their media buy.

Top Ad Networks

The following is a list of the top ad networks of 2014, as measured and ranked by comScore.

TOP COMSCORE RANKED PROPERTIES (2013)	UNIQUE VISITORS (1,000'S)	% REACH
GOOGLE AD NETWORK	209,314	94.1
CONVERSANT (FORMERLY VALUECLICK NETWORKS)	184,068	82.8
AT&T ADWORKS	183,548	82.5
ADVERTISING.COM	177,822	80.0
CRITEO	172,437	77.5
CASALE MEDIA - MEDIANET	171,919	77.3
MICROSOFT MEDIA NETWORK US	168,770	75.9
RADIUMONE	162,287	73.0
GENOME FROM YAHOO!	158,883	71.4
COLLECTIVE DISPLAY	157,277	70.7
BURST MEDIA	153,439	69.0
COX DIGITAL SOLUTIONS - NETWORK	150,986	67.9
SPECIFIC MEDIA	146,988	66.1
EXPONENTIAL - TRIBAL FUSION	145,590	65.5
ADCONION MEDIA GROUP	116,254	52.3
ROCKET FUEL	114,279	51.4
VIBRANT MEDIA	113,804	51.2
ZEDO ZINCX	100,690	45.3
SOURCEKNOWLEDGE VIDEO NETWORK	99,228	44.6
CPX INTERACTIVE	92,580	41.6

Purchasing Ad Network Inventory

Just as when purchasing inventory from publishers, media buyers contact the ad networks' sales departments to get proposals and to secure ad inventory. However, some ad networks offer a self-service platform that enables a media buyer to log in, select, and purchase media—without having to communicate with the sales department.

AD EXCHANGES

An ad exchange is an open-bid marketplace where premium publishers and ad networks sell their remnant and unsold inventory. Buying inventory from an ad exchange allows marketers to expand their reach beyond what ad networks can offer while still allowing them to buy ad space from multiple publishers through a single partner. Ad exchange inventory is sold at market price through an auction model, also known as real-time bidding (RTB).

Sample Ad Exchanges
Popular ad exchanges include, but are not limited to:

RUBICON	www.rubiconproject.com
ADMELD	www.admeld.com
ADBRITE	www.adbrite.com
PUBMATIC	www.pubmatic.com
RIGHT MEDIA	www.rightmedia.com
DOUBLECLICK	www.google.com/doubleclick
MICROSOFT ADVERTISING	www.advertising.microsoft.com/exchange
BID PLACE	www.bidplace.com
ADAP.TV	www.adap.tv
OPEN X	www.openx.com
LIJIT	www.lijit.com
APPNEXUS	www.appnexus.com
IMPROVE	www.improvedigital.com
CONTEXTWEB	www.contextweb.com

Purchasing via Ad Exchanges
There are two methods for purchasing media through an ad exchange: a demand-side platform (DSP) or a trading desk.

Demand Side Platforms (DSP)

A demand-side platform is a technology vendor that uses a proprietary algorithm to read, score, and bid on impressions, in real time, for an advertiser within the ad exchanges. DSP vendors include:

[X+1]	www.xplusone.com
LUCID MEDIA	www.lucidmedia.com
ROCKET FUEL	www.rocketfuel.com
NETMINING	www.netmining.com
INFLECTION POINT MEDIA	www.inflectionpointmedia.com
CONTEXTWEB	www.contextweb.com
INVITE MEDIA	www.invitemedia.com
OPTIM.AL	www.optim.al
TRIGGIT	www.triggit.com
CONVERSANT	www.conversantmedia.com
APPNEXUS	www.appnexus.com
RADIUM ONE	www.radiumone.com
SIMPLI.FI	www.simpli.fi
NETSHELTER	www.netshelter.com

Trading Desks

Trading desks are an agency's or holding company's department for dealing with DSPs. These agencies and holding companies partner with a DSP to license their algorithm to purchase inventory from the exchanges.

Whether working with a DSP or a trading desk, media buyers either contact the sales departments to secure inventory or use a self-service platform.

TARGETING

There are several ways to reach a desired audience across the Internet, with varied levels of targeting. These levels include run of media, inferred data, and registration data.

Run of Media

Run of media targeting can be the broadest form of targeting available and often does not use any targeting restrictions. All individuals who visit the designated website or network may be served the marketer's banner ad. Run of media targeting is used to build campaign scale because of its wide reach. Run of media is also the least expensive of the targeting methods because of its lack of restrictions.

Inferred Data

Inferred data targeting lets the marketer target more specifically by using intelligence gleaned from click, cookie, survey, or other deduced information to reach individuals who engage in a desired pattern of online behavior. Websites and networks anonymously track the online behavioral patterns of their visitors and identify the type of consumers that the marketer wants to reach.

Registration/Volunteered Data

Registration or volunteered data offers the most accurate form of targeting available. It uses defined information that is voluntarily given to a website by an individual. When websites require visitors to register before viewing or engaging with their online content, the data is captured and stored for use to later be appended with behaviors and other data they reveal to the site. The website is able to tell when that person logs in and can use the information previously provided to serve an appropriate ad. Common registration or volunteered data points include email address, age, gender and location.

TARGETING TACTICS

The three levels of targeting—run of media, behavioral data, and registration data—are further broken down into various targeting tactics.

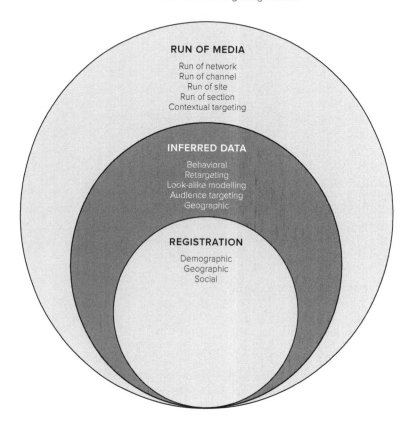

RUN OF MEDIA

Run of media is the broadest form of targeting, and there are several ways to implement it. Tactics include run of network, run of channel, run of site, run of section and contextual targeting. Typically, run of media targeting is used to align a brand with certain, desirable areas of content.

Run of Network

Run of network targeting is offered by ad networks. It reaches everyone who accesses any website across the entire network. For example, if a marketer purchases a run of network media buy, its banner ads will be served across the thousands of websites that are part of that network.

Run of Channel

Run of channel targeting is also offered by ad networks. In this form of targeting, websites within an ad network are grouped by contextual relevance. This allows a marketer to have its ads served across all the properties within the network that include relevant content. For example, instead of running media across all the sites in a network, a marketer may choose to only run on sports websites, also called the sports channel of the network. Run of channel may also be called content or contextual targeting.

Run of Site Targeting

Run of site targeting is offered by publishers. It reaches everyone who accesses any page on the publisher's website. For example, if a marketer purchases a run of site media buy, its ads will be served on all pages of the site, versus a specific page or section.

Run of Section

Run of section targeting is also offered by publishers. Similar to run of channel targeting, it allows marketers to select desirable content areas, versus having all sections of the website included in the media buy. For example, instead of running across a publisher's entire website, the marketer may choose to only run within the finance section of the site. Run of section may also be called content or contextual targeting.

Contextual Targeting

Contextual targeting allows marketers to target individuals who are viewing webpages containing relevant or desirable content. Websites and networks use algorithms to crawl webpages, find designated keywords, understand the context of the keyword within the webpage, then serve the marketer's banner ads if appropriate. For example, if an automobile brand purchases a contextually targeted media buy on a network, the brand will first build out a list of relevant keywords for its ads to show up against. These keywords may stem from search queries and may include words like "2013 model," "best car," or "auto reviews," as well as branded and competitive terms. Once the keyword list is developed, the ad network will run through all the websites in its network to find webpages where the selected keywords appear and show the automobile ads on those webpages, because the content is relevant to the campaign.

INFERRED DATA

Inferred data is information collected about web users based on their online behavior. Its resulting targeting tactics include behavioral targeting, retargeting, look-alike modeling and audience targeting.

Behavioral Targeting

Behavioral targeting allows a marketer to target its audience based on their online behavior. Websites and networks analyze the consumers' online habits (clicks, frequency, time spent, and types of websites visited) and serve an ad when someone demonstrates the behaviors that a marketing campaign is looking for. For example, when a marketer purchases a behaviorally targeted media buy on a website that does not have gated content, the website does not know the age, gender nor occupation of an individual who visits its pages. However, it can infer these details by following that individual's browsing habits. If the person reads articles about car reviews and motor shows, basketball games, and finance, plus looks at a market-data section, the website may infer that he is a male auto-enthusiast who works in finance. If the marketer is targeting that audience, its banner ad is served.

Retargeting

Retargeting allows marketers to target individuals who have already expressed interest by being exposed to or interacting with the brand. This brand exposure and interaction includes seeing a banner ad, visiting the brand's website, typing a search query, or taking an action on the website (such as a placing an item in a shopping cart, but not buying it). Retargeting keeps users in the brand embrace by following them around the Internet with appropriate and custom messaging. For example, when a shoe marketer purchases a retargeted media buy on an ad network, the ad network will track individuals who visit the shoe marketer's pages. If an individual looks at a pair of shoes, but does not buy them, retargeting will be able to reach that person again and serve them a reminder ad featuring the shoes they previously viewed with a compelling offer.

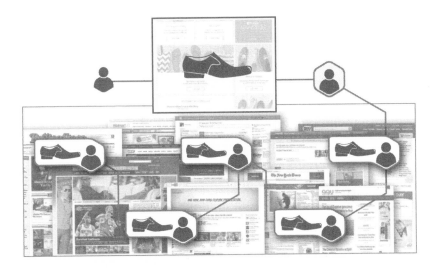

Look-alike Modeling

Look-alike modeling allows marketers to target individuals who "look like" their preferred audience. It finds consumers
who exhibit similar online patterns to those consumers who have already demonstrated a desired behavior, or who have
already generated a conversion on their site. A conversion is a marketing goal, such as a purchase, a completed form,
or downloaded content.

Websites and networks first build the data used in behavioral targeting, then use an algorithm to compute how similar an individual's online behavior is to the behaviors of other consumers who have already converted to target that individual appropriately. For example, when a marketer purchases look-alike modeling media on an ad network, the ad network will track individuals who have converted and follow them around the web. With its tracking and algorithm, it may see that sixty percent of conversions are from people who visit sports sites and live in New England. The ad network will then begin targeting other users who visit sports sites and live in New England because it has deduced that this is the look-alike audience.modeling media on an ad network, the ad network will track individuals who have converted and follow them around the web. With its tracking and algorithm, it may see that sixty percent of conversions are from people who visit sports sites and live in New England. The ad network will then begin targeting other users who visit sports sites and live in New England because it has deduced that this is the look-alike audience.

Audience Targeting

Audience targeting is a combination of targeting tactics rolled up into one line item within a media buy: behavioral, retargeting, contextual targeting, and demographic and geographic targeting. It is purchased from ad networks or DSPs and used to help marketers meet a specific goal. Instead of manually reallocating funds from one line item to another when optimizing a campaign, audience targeting allows ad networks and DSPs to automatically shift, in real-time, to whichever targeting tactic is driving the most conversions (i.e. clicks, sales, form completions, or downloads).

REGISTRATION/VOLUNTEERED DATA

Registration data is the most accurate form of targeting, and it is collected from information provided by users when registering for a website or adding additional information to their website profile. Targeting options include demographic, geographic, and social. While there are many websites and networks that require registration for members, for the purpose of this document, we will use Facebook as an example. However, many other sites have registration gateways for all or some of their content and features. These sites include, but are not limited to Match.com, the Wall Street Journal, Hulu and Twitter.

Demographic
Demographic targeting allows marketers to target individuals based on their demographic profiles. Some common demographic data include gender, age, and education level. For example, when a marketer purchases a demographic targeted media buy on a website, it is able to categorize which of its users meet the marketer's specifications for gender, age, and education level, and then serve the ads based on these demographics.

Geographic
Geographic targeting allows marketers to target people based on their location. Geographic data include countries, states, cities, and zip codes. For example, when a marketer purchases a geographically targeted media buy on a website, it is able to identify which of its users are located in a specific location, and then serve the ads based on these geographic selections.

Social
Social targeting allows marketers to target individuals based on their digital social connections and interests. Social connections include friends, fans, followers, connections, contacts, and other forms of social media relationships. For example, a company like Outdoor Center is able to target men based on a specific set of criteria that defines them as adults in New England, who
are interested in outdoor sports, and are not already a fan of Outdoor Center's Facebook page.

DEMOGRAPHIC	GEOGRAPHIC	CONNECTIONS	INTERESTS
+ Males, 18+	+ Vermont	Does not	+ Rock Climbing
	+ New Hampshire	currently like	+ Hiking
	+ Maine	Outdoor Center's	+ White Water Rafting
	+ Massachusetts	Facebook Page	+ Camping
	+ Connecticut		+ Skiing
	+ Rhode Island		+ Bike Riding

VIDEO

OVERVIEW

Digital video ads are clips that are typically 15, 30 or 60 seconds long. The video ads are either housed in a banner ad or played before, during, or after the viewing of a full-length video. Oftentimes, video ads are accompanied by companion ads to encourage clicks after the video is viewed.

AD FORMATS

Digital video may be used within any of the standard banner sizes, within custom sizes that are specific to individual publishers, and within video players on publishers' websites. Digital video placements may be classified as either in-banner or in-stream.

In-banner

In-banner placements are videos played within a standard banner. These videos may either be user-initiated (click-to-play) or auto-played. Video ads may also be part of rich-media ads.

In-stream

Similar to television commercials, in-stream video ads are auto-played within publishers' digital video content. Some in-stream ads give the viewer an option to skip it or just watch the first several seconds. Others require the viewer to watch it in its entirety before he or she can watch the original video content. Marketers may purchase three types of in-stream placements: pre-roll, mid-roll, or post-roll.

Pre-roll

A pre-roll placement is a video advertisement that is played before a publisher's video is viewed.

Mid-roll

A mid-roll placement is a video advertisement that is played as a commercial break during the viewing of a publisher's video.

Post-roll

A post-roll placement is a video advertisement that is played after the viewing of a publisher's video.

Sample Pre-Roll Video Ad

The above is an example of an in-stream pre-roll video ad. The video ad is being played prior to the start of the original video content selected by the individual. In some cases there is an option to close or skip the pre-roll ad before it completes. After the video ad is closed or viewed in its entirety, the original video content is then played.

COMPLEMENTARY VIDEO AD UNITS

There are other ad units that have been developed to accompany video content so marketers can boost their visibility on a video page and encourage clicks and conversions. These accompanying placements are often purchased as a package or sponsorship and may include one, or a combination, of the following ad units:

Companion Ads
A companion ad is a standard IAB banner that is shown on the same webpage while a video is playing.

In-stream Banners
In-stream banners are ads that are inserted within publishers' digital video content.

Overlays
An overlay ad is an image or text ad that is shown layered on top of the video while it is playing.

Skins
Skins are customizable and interchangeable background graphics for a webpage or a desktop.

Rails
Rails are wide skyscraper-style ads that line both the right and left side of a webpage.

Sample Pre-Roll and Companion Ad

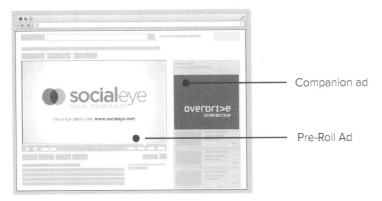

Companion ad

Pre-Roll Ad

The image above illustrates a pre-roll and a companion ad.

DIGITAL VIDEO VENDORS

A marketer's existing video files may be converted to digital-ready versions for ad placements through the use of rich media vendors. However, there are also video-specific vendors who specialize in selling and supporting video inventory. These digital video vendors include:

BRIGHTROLL	www.brightroll.com
YOUTUBE	www.youtube.com
SAY	www.saymedia.com
TUBEMOGUL	www.tubemogul.com
ADVECTION.NET	www.advection.net
BITGRAVITY	www.bitgravity.com
VIDEONAP	www.videonap.com
BREAK MEDIA	www.breakmedia.com
ADOTUBE	www.adotube.com
SPOTXCHANGE	www.spotexchange.com
CACHEFLY	www.cachefly.com
HULU	www.hulu.com
MOVE NETWORKS	www.movenetworks.com

MOBILE & TABLET

OVERVIEW

Advertising opportunities on mobile and tablet devices include banners on the mobile web, mobile applications, and location-based offers or coupons. The technology for mobile and tablet devices has been advancing at a rapid rate to accommodate virtually any capability that is currently offered in the desktop and laptop environments.

SIZES

MOBILE BANNER SIZES

Mobile ads are specially sized and designed for the compact screen of a smartphone. The ads appear when a user uses an app or visits a mobile site.

The image below shows examples of varying ad sizes that may be viewed on a mobile smartphone.

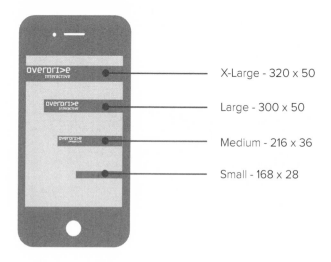

X-Large - 320 x 50

Large - 300 x 50

Medium - 216 x 36

Small - 168 x 28

TABLET BANNER SIZES

All sizes that are regularly available on desktops and laptops are also usually available on tablets, since these devices strive to provide a browser experience similar to a desktop or laptop.

The image below shows examples of ad sizes that may be viewed on a tablet device.

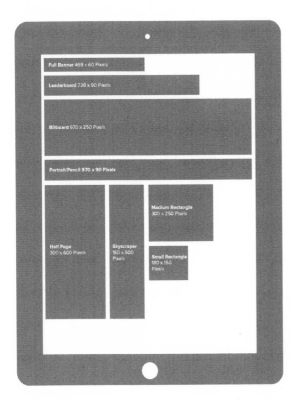

AD FORMATS

Like desktop and laptop ads, mobile and tablet ad formats are dictated by website specifications and the goal of the marketing. The most common types of formats include standard and mobile rich media.

STANDARD

Similar to desktop and laptop standard ads, mobile and tablet standard ads consist of any combination of static or animated imagery and text in a .jpg, .gif, or .png file. It is the most basic format and is the least expensive.

The image above shows a standard mobile banner, which only has one frame of copy and imagery.

MOBILE RICH MEDIA

Like desktop and laptop rich media ads, mobile and tablet rich media ads are designed to deliver virtually any online experience that a website or application can offer—all within the banner. It is the most high-impact format and it has the largest file size.

Rich Media Example

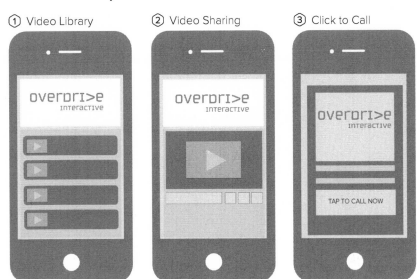

The image above shows a mobile rich media ad, which is promoting a library of videos. Users interacting with the ad can choose to watch a video, share a video on Facebook, or click to call for more information.

MOBILE RICH MEDIA VENDORS

There are several vendors that specialize in providing development software for marketers to create mobile rich media banners. Popular mobile rich media vendors include:

CELTRA	www.celtra.com
PHLUANT	www.phluant.com
AMBOBEE	www.amobee.com
CRISP MEDIA	www.crispmedia.com
MEDIALETS	www.medialets.com

MEASUREMENT & TRACKING

Similar to the measurement and tracking of desktop and laptop rich media ads, mobile rich media is able to track rich media engagement metrics, which include:

+ Time spent with the banner

+ Which parts of the banner were most focused on

+ Number of conversions

+ Number of closes or exits

+ Number of downloads

+ Number of leads captured

+ Number of shares

+ Video/play metrics

+ Survey/polling results

BUYING METHODS

Much like desktop and laptop ads, mobile ad inventory for websites and applications may be purchased through three types of media-distribution vendors: publisher direct, ad networks, and ad exchanges.

PUBLISHER DIRECT

A publisher is an individual website or organization that manages and disseminates content for public distribution or sale. Buying mobile and tablet inventory directly from publishers allows marketers to negotiate and purchase more premium media real estate, including content integration opportunities, sponsorships, and other unique offerings. Publishers include websites that focus on specific information such as news, entertainment, or sports.

AD NETWORKS

An ad network is an aggregator or broker of advertising inventory for many publishers. Buying mobile and tablet inventory from ad networks allows marketers to buy ad space from multiple publishers through a single partner. This buying method allows for extended reach and lower pricing. Popular mobile ad networks include:

ADMOB	www.admob.com
MILLENNIAL MEDIA	www.millennialmedia.com
ADFONIC	www.adfonic.com
SMAATO	www.smaato.com
INMOBI	www.inmobi.com
AMOBEE	www.amobee.com
ADMODA	www.admoda.com
MOBILEFUSE	www.mobilefuse.com
BUZZCITY	www.buzzcity.com
VELTI	www.velti.com
MOJIVA	www.mojiva.com

AD EXCHANGES

An ad exchange is an open bid marketplace where premium publishers and ad networks sell their remnant and unsold inventory. Buying inventory from an ad exchange allows marketers to expand their reach beyond what ad networks can offer while still allowing them to buy ad space from multiple publishers through a single partner. Ad exchange inventory is sold at market price through an auction model. Popular mobile ad exchanges include:

DATA XU	www.dataxu.com
STRIKEAD	www.strikead.com
DSNR MEDIA GROUP	www.dsnrmg.com
OPERA	www.opera.com
CEVA	www.ceva-dsp.com

TARGETING

Mobile advertising is best known for its geographic targeting capabilities. However, like desktop and laptop advertising, mobile advertising is also able to reach a desired audience using run of media, inferred data, and registration data.

The key difference between mobile targeting and desktop and laptop targeting is the ability to target by mobile or tablet device. Targeting by device is necessary within the mobile and tablet environment because each device has different ad specifications and internet capabilities. Marketers need to create different ad sizes to be compatible with each targeted device.

For example, if the banner ad is promoting an iPhone only app, the marketer must ensure that they are only advertising on devices that support their product.

Mobile Operating System Targeting

SOCIAL ADS

OVERVIEW

Social media publishers offer many advertising products, from standard banners to interactive polls. For the purposes of this document, a social ad is any ad that appears on a social media website and encourages a social response or interaction. Social ads are often defined by one or more of the following characteristics:

Social Functionality
Social functionality within ads encourages users to like, share, connect with brands, become a member of a group, or register for a website.

Embedded in Social Content
When an ad is embedded in social content, it appears in an individual's social media feed or on the homepage dashboard.

Social Targeting
Ads on social media sites may be custom targeted because social properties are a gold mine of user registration data. The wealth of information shared by registered users allows advertisers to use a unique set of targeting methods.

While most social media platforms offer advertising opportunities, this section will focus on three of the most popular social networks: Facebook, Twitter, and LinkedIn. These properties offer clear examples of how social media contributes to the display media landscape.

FACEBOOK

Due to the amount of information users share every day, Facebook has a vast collection of registration and volunteered data. As users post content, update their status, navigate Facebook and the web—liking pages, sharing content, and live-streaming their playlists—data is collected and used for niche media targeting.

Facebook does not display or sell standard IAB banner sizes, but instead sells proprietary ad placements including desktop and mobile News Feed ads, right rail ads on desktop and logout screen ads. As Facebook ads products are constantly changing and evolving, the ad placements below are current as of April 2014.

FACEBOOK AD FORMATS

Right Rail and News Feed Ads

Right Rail ads are a combination of text and imagery that appear on the right-hand side of the homepage. They may be used to either promote likes of a brand's page or to drive users outside of Facebook to a brand's website.

News Feed ads are stories that are shown to users about their friends' interactions with a brand. They are displayed directly within the News Feed and used to promote actions such as share, like, or comment.

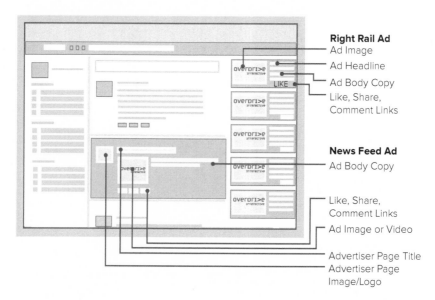

Right Rail Ad
Ad Image
Ad Headline
Ad Body Copy
Like, Share, Comment Links

News Feed Ad
Ad Body Copy

Like, Share, Comment Links
Ad Image or Video

Advertiser Page Title
Advertiser Page Image/Logo

Mobile Ads

Mobile News Feed ads and mobile page ads will be served on m.facebook.com and on native iOS and Android applications.

Mobile
News Feed Ad

Logout Screen Ads

A logout screen ad is a wide-format banner that is served after a user logs out of his Facebook account. This is Facebook's largest and most expensive ad format, and it is usually sold in a bundle with other ads.

TWITTER

Like Facebook, Twitter does not display or sell standard IAB banner sizes. It too offers niche targeting tactics based on its rich registration and volunteered data, which includes tweet topics and other users followed. Twitter sells proprietary ad placements including promoted accounts, promoted tweets, and promoted trends. The ad formats outlined below are accurate as of April 14, 2014, and are expected to change over time as new and improved ad products are developed.

TWITTER AD FORMATS

Promoted Tweets
The promoted tweet for Overdrive appears in a user's timeline or on search results, and is identified as an advertisement by the yellow arrow and the word "Promoted." It is targeted to users based on keywords.

Promoted Accounts
In the example above, the promoted accounts ad for Overdrive is seen under the "Who To Follow" section and is identified as an advertisement by the yellow arrow. It is being served because the user has been identified with the targeted interests or user accounts Overdrive has designated for its campaign.

Promoted Trends
Promoted trends help marketers generate awareness, buzz, and conversation about specific topics. Twitter allows only one such advertiser per day. It is similar in scale and impact to a homepage takeover and has a very high daily cost. However, the potential volume received from purchasing promoted trends may make it very cost-effective and efficient for building awareness. They are targeted to users based on keywords.

LINKEDIN

LinkedIn is a social media destination that encourages members to build profiles and expand their professional networks. Member's profiles are virtual resumes. Like Facebook, LinkedIn has a vast collection of registration and volunteered data. As users join groups, participate in discussions, update their resumes, and subscribe to company profiles, data is collected and used for media targeting.

AD FORMATS

LinkedIn sells ad inventory for standard IAB banner sizes, which run throughout the site. These banners accommodate standard, Flash, and rich-media content. In addition to these banners, LinkedIn also sells sponsored polls, text ads, InMail messages, sponsored updates, follow company ads and more.

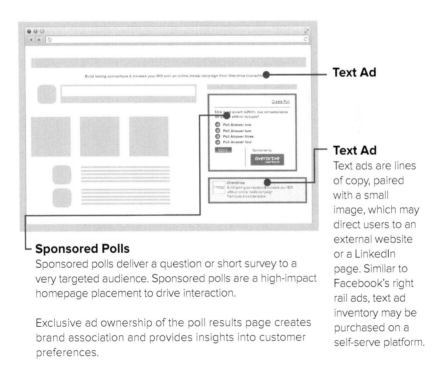

Text Ad

Text Ad
Text ads are lines of copy, paired with a small image, which may direct users to an external website or a LinkedIn page. Similar to Facebook's right rail ads, text ad inventory may be purchased on a self-serve platform.

Sponsored Polls
Sponsored polls deliver a question or short survey to a very targeted audience. Sponsored polls are a high-impact homepage placement to drive interaction.

Exclusive ad ownership of the poll results page creates brand association and provides insights into customer preferences.

Sponsored polls are usually bundled with display banner ads.

InMail Messages

InMail messages deliver relevant messages to specific audiences or a targeted group of LinkedIn members. Marketers who purchase InMail are ensured that it is delivered top the top of a LinkedIn member's inbox.

Members only receive one InMail message per 60 days, giving the marketer impact and exclusivity.

Standard IAB Banner Sizes

LinkedIn sells standard IAB banners sizes, specifically 728x90 leaderboards, 300x250 rectangles, and 120x600 skyscrapers.

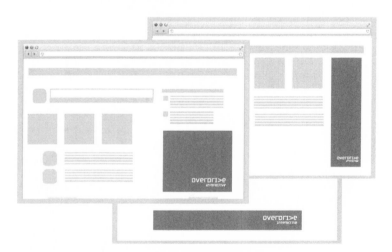

INFORMATION IS CURRENT AS OF THE PUBLISING DATE.

Follow Company Ads

Follow company ads are 300x250 standard banners that are used to gain new followers of a company's LinkedIn page. Marketers typically purchase this ad to build a larger volume of professionals interested in their company.

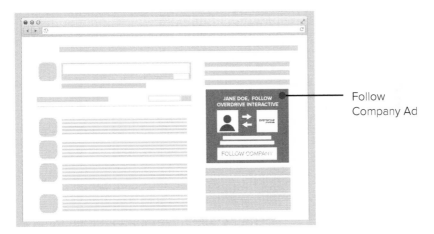

Follow Company Ad

Sponsored Updates

Sponsored Updates allow advertisers to promote organic status updates using the same targeting parameters as other LinkedIn ads. Ads appear in the user's news feed, alongside organic content.

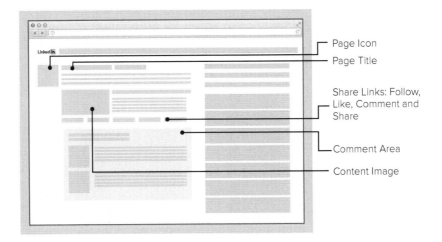

Page Icon

Page Title

Share Links: Follow, Like, Comment and Share

Comment Area

Content Image

PAID SEARCH ADS

PAID SEARCH ADS

Paid Search Ads

Search ads are text-based ads that typically appear within Google, Bing or Yahoo! search results. They are used to place a brand's message at the critical moment when a consumer is actively looking for a particular brand or solution via keyword search. Search ads are purchased on a real-time auction bid on a cost-per-click (CPC) basis. The cost of the click is determined by the competitiveness and relevancy to the user, based on the particular search term being purchased in the keyword auction marketplace.

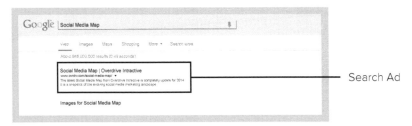
Search Ad

In the example above, a relevant search ad is delivered against a Google search query.

Paid search ads have a character limit for each line of the ad. Different search engines have different character lengths, but, in general, there are four lines that you can influence.

	EXAMPLE AD	MAX LENGTH (MOST LANGUAGES	LENGTH (DOUBLE-WIDTH * LANGUAGES)
HEADLINE	EXAMPLE WEBSITE	25 CHARACTERS	12 CHARACTERS
DESCRIPTION LINE 1	SUMMER SALE	35 CHARACTERS	17 CHARACTERS
DESCRIPTION LINE 2	SAVE 15%	35 CHARACTERS	17 CHARACTERS
DISPLAY URL	WWW. EXAMPLE .COM	35 CHARACTERS	17 CHARACTERS

*Double-width languages are languages that use double-width characters, like Chinese, Japanese, and Korean.

AD EXTENSIONS

Ad extensions are features that may be appended to the end of a search ad, which allow a brand to promote certain information upfront such as an address, phone number, links to other pages of a website, or a special offer. Different extensions may come and go as the search engines update, test and enhance features. Typically, there is no additional cost to apply ad extensions, but click charges may apply when they are utilized by a user.

Sitelink Ad Extensions
Sitelink ad extensions are search ads that have up to four URLs appended to the end. They are used to drive consumers directly to deeper pages of a website.

Sitelinks Ad
Extension

Location Ad Extensions
Location ad extensions are search ads that have an address and phone number appended to the end, underneath the URL. They are typically used to drive consumers offline and into a nearby store.

Location Ad
Extension

In the example above, a location ad extension appears below the search ad, following a Google search query.

Call Ad Extensions

Call ad extensions are search ads that drive consumers to call a brand directly. Similar to location ad extensions, a phone number is appended to the end, underneath the URL, when served on a desktop or laptop device. When served on a mobile device, a click to call button is appended to the end instead.

Call Ad Extension

In the example above, a call ad extension appears below the search ad, following a Google search query on a mobile device.

Offer Ad Extensions

Offer ad extensions are search ads that have a discount offer or coupon appended to the end, underneath the URL. They are typically used to drive consumers offline and into a nearby store.

Offer Ad Extension

Product Listing Ads (PLAs)

Product listing ads (PLAs) are search ads that have featured products appended to the end, underneath the URL. They are used to highlight products that are already listed under a brand's Google Merchant Center (GMC) account. Since the products featured are specific to the GMC, an advertiser must have an active AdWords and GMC account and be conducting ecommerce on its site. These ad extensions may appear with images of the products or as simple text-based lists.

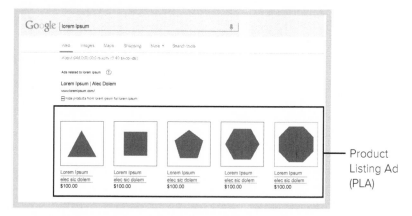

Product Listing Ad (PLA)

In the example above, a product listing ad (PLA) with images appears below the search ad, following a Google search query.

Social Ad Extensions

Social ad extensions are search ads that have the number of people that have followed the brand or +1'd in Google+ appended to the end, underneath the URL. Clicking the +1 link adds another fan count to the brand's Google+ page.

Social Ad Extension

In the example above, a social ad extension appears below the search ad, following a Google search query.

Communication Ad Extensions

Communication ad extensions are search ads that have a one-step form appended to the end, underneath the URL. They allow consumers to sign up for alerts, updates and offers directly at the ad level, without being directed away from their original search query. The form data is captured by Google and delivered directly to the brand. Available entries for the form are email, zip code or name and are followed by a "Privacy" link to inform consumers that their information will be shared with the brand.

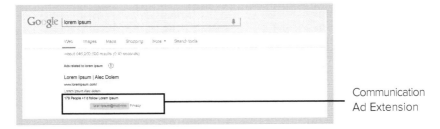

Communication
Ad Extension

In the example above, a communication ad extension, which requests consumers sign up for a newsletter, has been appended to the search ad.

App Ad Extensions

App ad extensions are search ads that have a promotional call-out for a mobile or tablet app, which are appended to the end, underneath the URL. New users are sent directly to the app store to download the app, while existing users may be sent to a specific page within the app to complete a conversion.

App Ad Extension

OTHER MEDIA

OVERVIEW

Other types of digital media include whitepaper syndication programs, virtual conferences, sponsored webinars, emails, newsletter sponsorships, text ads, and text links. These formats are most commonly used for business-to-business (B2B) lead-generation campaigns, but business-to-consumer (B2C) campaigns can also benefit from these placements.

WHITEPAPER AND CONTENT SYNDICATION

Whitepaper syndication networks are media organizations that consolidate various marketing assets such as whitepapers, case studies, podcasts, webinars, and videos into content libraries. These assets are then pushed out to other sites, or are promoted on their own properties within the network. These networks act as huge content and whitepaper databases that power the whitepaper libraries of other sites.

Marketers and media buyers use whitepaper syndication to generate leads. A whitepaper syndication program is typically used by technology companies seeking a B2B audience. The whitepaper syndication network or website will often guarantee a certain number of qualified leads, so leads can be purchased on a cost-per-lead (CPL) basis. The leads get more expensive as the buyer requests more targeting selections, called lead filters, which may include geography, industry, job title or level, and company size. The network or website captures lead data from interested individuals who wish to download the marketer's promoted asset. Afterward, all qualified leads are sent to the marketer until the lead guarantee is met.

Sample Whitepaper Syndication Networks
Below are examples of whitepaper syndication networks for a tech B2B campaign:

MADISON LOGIC	www.madisonlogic.com
CBS INTERACTIVE	www.cbsinteractive.com
EMEDIA	www.emedia.com
TECH TARGET	www.techtarget.com
IDG CONNECT	www.idgconnect.com
IDG TECH NETWORK	www.idgtechnetwork.com
ZIFF DAVIS ENTERPRISE	www.ziffdavisenterprise.com
TOOLBOX	www.toolbox.com

HOW WHITEPAPER SYNDICATION WORKS

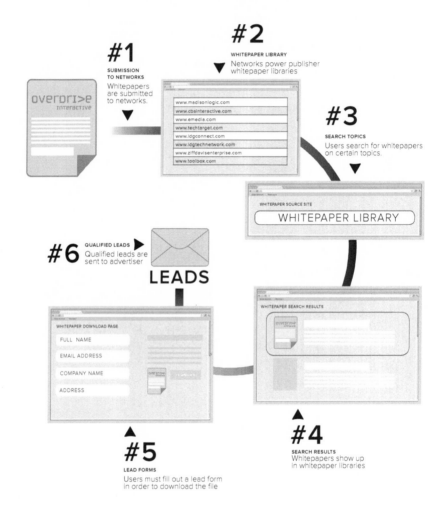

#1

SUBMISSION TO NETWORKS
Whitepapers are submitted to networks.

#2

WHITEPAPER LIBRARY
Networks power publisher whitepaper libraries

www.madisonlogic.com
www.cbsinteractive.com
www.emedia.com
www.techtarget.com
www.idgconnect.com
www.idgtechnetwork.com
www.ziffdavisenterprise.com
www.toolbox.com

#3

SEARCH TOPICS
Users search for whitepapers on certain topics.

WHITEPAPER SOURCE SITE

WHITEPAPER LIBRARY

#6

QUALIFIED LEADS
Qualified leads are sent to advertiser

LEADS

WHITEPAPER SEARCH RESULTS

WHITEPAPER DOWNLOAD PAGE

FULL NAME

EMAIL ADDRESS

COMPANY NAME

ADDRESS

#5

LEAD FORMS
Users must fill out a lead form in order to download the file

#4

SEARCH RESULTS
Whitepapers show up in whitepaper libraries

VIRTUAL CONFERENCES

Much like at live conferences, in a virtual conference, marketers can build a virtual booth for their brand or organization. Virtual booths include branding collateral such as booth design and banners, as well as takeaways like whitepapers, case studies, and videos.

Virtual conferences may include a presentation by a company representative, which is then followed by a real-time question-and-answer session to better engage with the participants. Participants are also offered the option to download various assets. Marketers typically receive leads from the virtual conference organizers as they capture lead information from conference attendees.

Virtual conferences are used for both lead-generation and brand-awareness campaigns and are usually purchased at a flat rate or as a package deal.

In the example above, an Overdrive virtual conference is being held to promote all of the agency's capabilities. A conference attendee may click to watch the video or review the content pages that are listed along the right-hand side of the screen. He may also chat with a live representative.

DEDICATED EMAILS

A dedicated email is a custom email that is sent to a publisher's list of subscribers. Each dedicated email is entirely devoted to a single marketer. It allows marketers to reach a specific target audience by leveraging a website subscriber base. Dedicated emails contain direct calls to action and multiple links to a landing page.

Dedicated emails are used for longevity in the digital space as they typically remain in the user's inbox for some time, and they can be re-read and forwarded. They are usually purchased at a flat rate or on a per-send basis.

In the example above, the Overdrive dedicated email would be sent out to a publisher's list of subscribers.

NEWSLETTER SPONSORSHIPS

A newsletter sponsorship is an ad placement in a publisher's newsletter, which is sent out to its subscribers. Newsletter sponsorships allow a marketer to align its ads with a specific topic and reach a targeted audience. Ad placements for a newsletter sponsorship include banner ads, text ads, text links, and logo inclusions.

Like dedicated emails, newsletter sponsorships also offer longevity and are usually purchased at a flat rate or on a per-send basis.

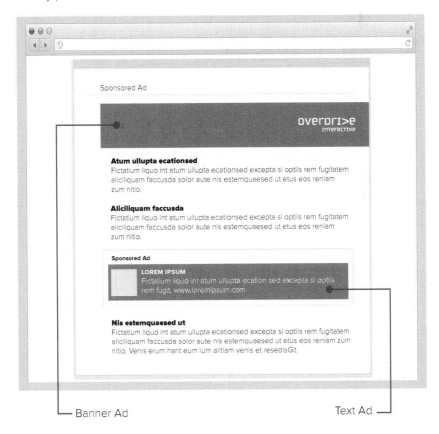

Banner Ad

Text Ad

In the example above, an Overdrive banner is inserted into a publisher's newsletter to gain exposure among its subscribers.

T E X T   A D S

Text Link Ads

Text links are all text ads that appear on the peripherals of websites or as a placement within a newsletter sponsorship.

In the example above, a text link appears at the top of the page on LinkedIn.

Vibrant Media or Kontera's in-text ads may also be considered text ads. These ads appear over the content of a webpage when an individual rolls over a word that has been double-underlined in green.

① Before Rollover

② After Rollover

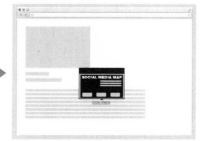

In this example, Overdrive has designed a campaign to promote its social media map. It has built a targeted keyword list of relevant terms it would like Vibrant or Kontera to find and target, which includes the term "social media." Since social media is being discussed in the article, the term has been double-underlined in green to signify that a user may roll over it to see an ad.

Upon hovering over the keyword "social media," Overdrive's ad promoting its social media map appears as a pop-up window, over the content of the webpage.

PRICING MODELS

OVERVIEW

The cost of inventory is determined through six main pricing models: fixed-rates, cost-per-click (CPC), cost-per-thousand impressions (CPM), cost-per-action (CPA), cost-per-sale (CPS), or real-time-bidding (RTB).

PRICING MODELS

PRICING MODEL	FORMULA	USE
FIXED-RATE	Spend is a hard cost set by the vendor	Fixed rates are often used for sponsorships, content syndication, and other premium media placements.
CPM: COST-PER-THOUSAND IMPRESSIONS	Cost = impressions x CPM rate / 1,000	The standard pricing model, CPM may be used across media channels for easy comparison.
CPC: COST-PER-CLICK	Cost = clicks x CPC rate	CPC allows a brand to receive as many impressions as necessary in order to fulfill a desired click-response goal.
CPA: COST-PER-ACTION	Cost = actions x CPA rate	CPA allows a brand to receive as many impressions as necessary in order to fulfill a desired acquisition goal (leads, orders, actions, etc.)
CPS: COST-PER-SALE	Cost = sales x CPS rate	CPS allows a brand to receive as many impressions as necessary in order to fulfill a desired sales goal.
RTB: REAL TIME BIDDING	Cost fluctuates with competitive bids	RTB enables a brand to pay market value per impression or click, gaining maximum control over the price of media.

AD SERVING

OVERVIEW

Advertising agencies typically use a third-party ad server to manage their media. Those who do not use ad servers either have their own proprietary serving method or use rudimentary and manual processes, which requires that they send assets directly to each and every media vendor and painstakingly gather the results.

AD SERVER

An ad server is a technology platform that allows for the management and tracking of all digital campaigns. Popular ad server vendors include, but are not limited to:

ADREADY	www.adready.com
ZEDO	www.zedo.com
CONVERSANT	www.conversantmedia.com
BRIGHTCOVE	www.brightcove.com
ADVERTISING.COM	www.advertising.com
DOUBLECLICK	www.google.com/doubleclick
POINTROLL	www.pointroll.com
HIRO	www.hiromedia.com
ATLAS	www.atlassolutions.com
OPEN X	www.openx.com

AD SERVER MEDIA MANAGEMENT

Ad servers allow media managers to set up campaigns, make changes, and react in real time to campaign performance. Through an ad server, media managers are able to control which sites, media placements, or creative materials are active, paused, or scheduled. They can manage different creative rotations within a given placement and specify different landing pages for each. This is all managed and consolidated on the back end—without having to contact each property individually to make each change.

HOW AD SERVERS WORK

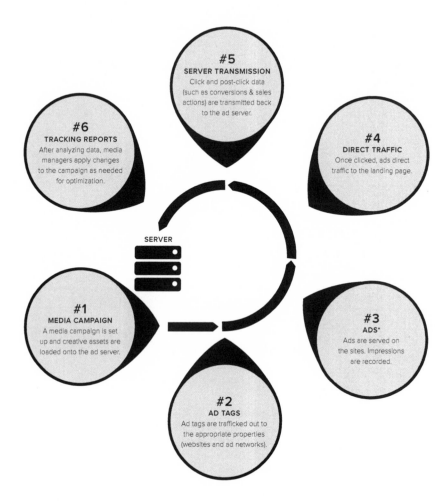

#5
SERVER TRANSMISSION
Click and post-click data
(such as conversions & sales
actions) are transmitted back
to the ad server.

#6
TRACKING REPORTS
After analyzing data, media
managers apply changes
to the campaign as needed
for optimization.

#4
DIRECT TRAFFIC
Once clicked, ads direct
traffic to the landing page.

SERVER

#1
MEDIA CAMPAIGN
A media campaign is set
up and creative assets are
loaded onto the ad server.

#3
ADS*
Ads are served on
the sites. Impressions
are recorded.

#2
AD TAGS
Ad tags are trafficked out to
the appropriate properties
(websites and ad networks).

* Ads served through an ad server may either be banners, dedicated emails, text
links or text ads.

ROI & OPTIMIZATION

ROI & OPTIMIZATION

AD SERVER REPORTING

Ad servers provide extensive tracking data, which media managers rely on to optimize campaigns. Metrics such as spend, impressions served, clicks, visits to landing pages, and conversions are collected by the ad server and delivered as raw data or pre-formatted reports.

The optimization process occurs when media managers use tracking data to make real-time changes to digital campaigns. Ad servers offer media dashboards and reports that include information such as topline reports, detailed reports, and creative reports.

Sample Topline Report

Site Name	Impressions	Clicks	Click Rate	CPM	CPC	Media Cost	Actions	Cost-per-action	Conversion Rate
Site 1	728,795	1,650	0.23%	$5.37	$2.37	$3,915.74	243	$16.11	14.73%
Site 2	875,165	1,706	0.19%	$8.00	$4.10	$7,000.00	303	$23.10	17.76%
Site 3	3,960,676	4,276	0.11%	$2.59	$2.40	$10,275.00	2,272	$4.52	53.13%
Site 4	1,601,545	2,844	0.18%	$5.48	$3.09	$8,774.39	1,843	$4.76	64.80%
Network 1	691,220	1,193	0.17%	$7.58	$4.39	$5,242.47	613	$8.55	51.39%
Network 2	1,888,323	1,830	0.10%	$4.18	$4.32	$7,900.00	446	$17.71	24.37%
Network 3	10,188,102	3,866	0.04%	$3.42	$9.00	$34,800.00	1,340	$25.97	34.66%
Campaign Total/Avgs	**19,993,826**	**17,365**	**0.09%**	**$3.91**	**$4.49**	**$77,907.60**	**7,060**	**$11.04**	**40.66%**

Topline reports provide a bird's-eye view of media campaigns. These reports show site-level activity and are often used to check in on active campaigns to ensure that everything is running smoothly or quickly spot media that is not performing.
The ease of compiling topline reports during a campaign also facilitates rapid adjustments to optimize the campaign.

Sample Detailed Report

Site Name	Placement Name	Impressions	Clicks	Click Rate	CPM	CPC	Medi
Site 1	Placement A	56,809	301	0.53%	$0.00	$0.00	$0.00
Site 1	Placement B	57,189	347	0.61%	$0.00	$0.00	$0.00
Site 1	Placement C	119,048	260	0.22%	$5.04	$2.31	$600.00
Site 1	Placement D	264,468	393	0.15%	$8.00	$5.38	$2,115.74
Site 1	Placement E	122,911	209	0.17%	$4.88	$2.87	$600.00
Site 1	Placement F	108,370	140	0.13%	$5.54	$4.29	$600.00
Site 1 Totals/Avgs		**728,795**	**1,650**	**0.23%**	**$5.37**	**$2.37**	**$3,915.7**
Site 2	Placement A	500,075	1,031	0.21%	$8.00	$3.88	$4,000.0
Site 2	Placement B	375,090	675	0.18%	$8.00	$4.44	$3,000.0
Site 2 Totals/Avgs		**875,165**	**1,706**	**0.19%**	**$8.00**	**$4.10**	**$7,000.0**
Site 3	Placement A	474,349	585	0.12%	$8.54	$6.92	$4,050.0
Site 3	Placement B	769,540	779	0.10%	$3.41	$3.37	$2,625.0
Site 3	Placement C	1,465,440	1,385	0.10%	$2.46	$2.36	$3,600.0
Site 3	Placement D	1,251,347	1,385	0.11%	$0.00	$0.00	$0.00
Site 3 Totals/Avgs		**3,960,679**	**4,276**	**0.11%**	**$2.59**	**$2.40**	**$10,275.**
Site 4	Placement A	93,899	252	0.27%	$4.26	$1.59	$400.00
Site 4	Placement B	1,160,426	1,896	0.16%	$5.00	$3.06	$5,800.0
Site 4	Placement C	275,298	564	0.20%	$7.00	$3.42	$1,927.09
Site 4	Placement D	71,922	132	0.18%	$9.00	$4.90	$647.30
Site 4 Totals/Avgs		**1,601,545**	**2,844**	**0.18%**	**$5.48**	**$3.09**	**$8,774.3**
Network 1	Placement A	121,694	386	0.32%	$7.95	$2.51	$967.47
Network 1	Placement B	286,884	412	0.14%	$7.93	$5.52	$2,275.0
Network 1	Placement C	282,642	395	0.14%	$7.08	$5.06	$2,000.0
Network 1 Totals/Avgs		**691,220**	**1,193**	**0.17%**	**$7.08**	**$4.39**	**$5,242.4**
Network 2	Placement A	1,223,822	1,127	0.09%	$3.68	$3.99	$4,500.0
Network 2	Placement B	664,501	703	0.11%	$5.12	$4.84	$3,400.0
Network 2 Totals/Avgs		**1,888,323**	**1,830**	**0.10%**	**$4.18**	**$4.32**	**$7,900.0**
Network 3	Placement A	113,353	49	0.04%	$0.00	$0.00	$0.00
Network 3	Placement B	154,929	58	0.04%	$0.00	$0.00	$0.00
Network 3	Placement C	5,126,317	1,282	0.03%	$3.39	$13.57	$17,400.0
Network 3	Placement D	4,793,503	2,477	0.05%	$3.63	$7.02	$17,400.0
Network 3 Total Avgs		**10,188,102**	**3,866**	**0.04%**	**$3.42**	**$9.00**	**$34,800.**
Campaign Total/Avgs		**19,993,826**	**17,365**	**0.09%**	**$3.91**	**$4.49**	**$77,907.6**

ions	Cost-per-action	Conversion Rate
	$0.00	11.30%
	$0.00	7.78%
	$12.50	18.46%
	$31.58	17.05%
	$13.64	21.05%
	$26.09	16.43%
	$16.11	**14.73%**
	$17.39	22.31%
	$41.10	10.81%
	$23.10	**17.76%**
	$12.16	56.92%
	$8.10	41.59%
	$3.88	60.84%
	$0.00	49.53%
72	**$4.52**	**53.13%**
	$3.01	52.78%
7	$4.04	75.79%
	$8.10	42.20%
	$18.49	26.52%
43	**$4.76**	**64.80%**
	$9.30	26.94%
	$10.07	54.85%
	$7.07	71.65%
	$8.55	**51.38%**
	$19.47	20.23%
	$15.60	31.01%
	$17.71	**24.37%**
	$0.00	83.67%
	$0.00	65.52%
	$24.13	56.24%
	$32.22	21.80%
40	**$32.22**	**34.66%**
60	**$11.04**	**40.66%**

Sample Detailed Report

Detailed reports outline campaign performance by property and by placement. They are often provided on a weekly or monthly basis to accurately interpret trends in the data. Placements with poor conversion rates or inflated CPAs can be paused to shift media funds toward better-performing placements. In the sample report above, Placement B on Site 2 would be canceled due to its poor conversion rate, while Placement B on Site 4 would receive additional funds since it has a much stronger conversion rate. This reallocation process is what online marketers refer to as "optimization."

Creative and Ad Unit Reports

Serving banner creative via an ad server also enables marketers to generate reports with accurate campaign metrics for each creative. This allows marketers to accurately assess the performance of various messages and offers. The same can be said for placement size and a host of other elements.

Creative Concept	Impressions	Clicks	Click Rate	CPM	CPC	Media Cost	Actions	Cost-per-action	Conversion Rate
Creative A	9,966,332	8,738	0.09%	$3.91	$4.46	$38,994.02	3,370	$11.57	39%
Creative B	9,967,494	8,627	0.09%	$3.90	$4.51	$38,913.58	4,891	$7.96	57%
Campaign Total/Avgs	19,993,826	17,365	0.09%	$3.91	$4.49	$77,907.60	7,060	$11.04	40.66%

In the sample report above, creative concept B has a significantly higher conversion rate as well as a lower cost-per-action. Therefore, the media manager should reallocate more impressions to Concept B.

Creative Concept	Impressions	Clicks	Click Rate	CPM	CPC	Media Cost	Actions	Cost-per-action	Conver-sion Rate
160 x 600	1,791,740	2,088	0.12%	$2.57	$2.20	$4,600.00	1,151	$4.00	55.12%
300 x 250	7,801,331	6,821	0.09%	$4.50	$5.15	$35,123.87	1,965	$17.87	28.81%
300 x 250	1,655,721	2,291	0.14%	$5.17	$3.80	$8,708.55	606	$14.37	26.45%
728 x 90	8,655,034	6,165	0.07%	$3.41	$4.78	$29,475.19	3,338	$8.83	54.14%
Campaign Total/Avgs	19,993,826	17,365	0.09%	$3.91	$4.49	$77,907.60	7,060	$11.04	40.66%

In the sample report above, the leaderboard (728x90) and the skyscraper (160x600) generated the highest conversion rates and the lowest cost-per-action. Therefore, the media manager should reallocate more impressions to these better-performing sizes to enhance campaign performance.

ATTRIBUTION MODELING

OVERVIEW

Attribution modeling is a reporting model that allows marketers to understand a consumer's path to conversion. It shows how each media channel, vendor, and targeting tactic contributes to driving a consumer through the conversion funnel to apportion media ROI by the percentage of credit that is deserved. The different types of attribution modeling include lower funnel, full funnel, and cross channel.

LOWER-FUNNEL ATTRIBUTION

Lower-funnel attribution, also known as click-based attribution, studies the last click that drove a conversion, but it does not take into account the assisting clicks along the way. This model provides a strong sense of how well click-based media are working because it looks at the customer's last touch point (i.e. click) before conversion. However, lower-funnel attribution does not always provide a strong case for display media, which relies heavily on viewing metrics (i.e. impressions).

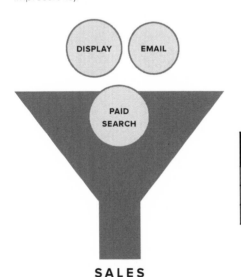

MEDIA CHANNEL	ATTRIBUTION OF SALES
PAID SEARCH	$100
DISPLAY	$0
EMAIL	$0

In the example above, the last media channel that the consumer interacted with before converting was paid search (this was done by clicking on a paid search ad after a search query). Therefore, paid search gets the full credit for the conversion.

FULL-FUNNEL ATTRIBUTION

Unlike lower-funnel attribution, full-funnel attribution incorporates impressions and assisted clicks in a conversion. It looks at the full path to conversion and does not just focus on the last touch point (i.e. click).

With full-funnel attribution, credit may be given to a media tactic that may not have delivered a high volume of direct click conversions, but delivered a measurable impact on branding and sales during the purchase consideration phase.

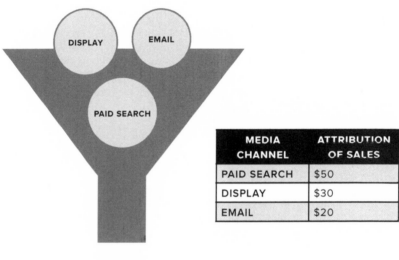

MEDIA CHANNEL	ATTRIBUTION OF SALES
PAID SEARCH	$50
DISPLAY	$30
EMAIL	$20

SALES
$100

In the example above, a marketer is using paid search, email and display for a campaign. Looking at the full path to conversion, the last media channel the consumer interacted with before converting was paid search (this was done by clicking on a paid search ad after a search query). However, the consumer has also seen a display banner and read an email prior to the search query. Therefore, while paid search gets the majority of the credit for the conversion, display and email will get partial credit for assisting the conversion.

CROSS-CHANNEL ATTRIBUTION

Like full-funnel attribution, cross-channel attribution does not just focus on the last touch point (i.e. click). It looks at all
the media channels and considers the full path to conversion. Cross-channel attribution helps marketers understand the level of spend each channel should get in order to drive the best results. By building out a model, a marketer is able to apply different budget scenarios to better understand the outcome of all its marketing efforts and plan accordingly.

Other media channels may include print, direct response, radio, television, and out-of-home advertising. If lift is seen by an offline channel, ROI may be apportioned and credited based on the level of lift.

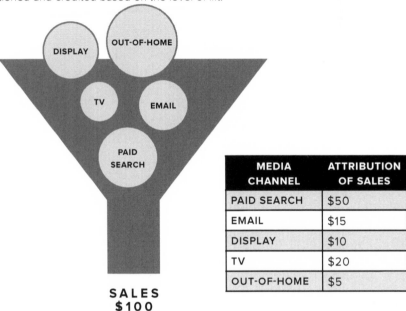

MEDIA CHANNEL	ATTRIBUTION OF SALES
PAID SEARCH	$50
EMAIL	$15
DISPLAY	$10
TV	$20
OUT-OF-HOME	$5

SALES $100

In the example above, a marketer is using paid search, email, display, television, and out-of-home for a campaign. The last media channel that the consumer interacted with before converting was paid search (this was done by clicking on a paid search ad after a search query). However, the consumer has also seen a television commercial, an out-of-home billboard, a display banner, and read an email prior to the search query. Therefore, while paid search gets the majority of the credit for the conversion, television, out-of-home, display and email will also get partial credit for assisting the conversion.

ATTRIBUTION REPORTING

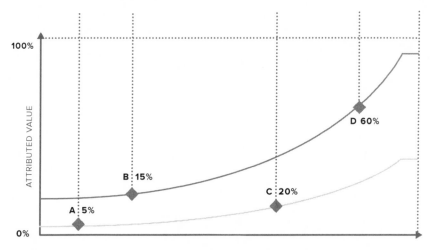

KEY

A = DISPLAY IMPRESSION

B = DISPLAY CLICK

C = DISPLAY IMPRESSION

D = SEARCH CLICK

— CLICKS

— IMPRESSIONS

In the graph above, every media touch-point along a consumer's path to conversion has been given a partial value based on its contribution towards the sale: A + B + C + D = 100%. Though an individual may have converted directly from a search click, he was influenced to convert by first seeing a banner (A) and clicking on it (B), then seeing another banner (C). Since the first banner impression seen was the farthest away from the conversion action, it has been given the lowest weight.

The search click, which ultimately drove the conversion, has been given the most weight.

MEDIA GLOSSARY

G L O S S A R Y

AD DISPLAY/ AD DELIVERY:
When an ad is successfully displayed on a digital screen.

AD DOWNLOAD:
When a server successfully delivers the ad onto the user's browser. Ads can be requested, but aborted or abandoned before actually being downloaded to the browser.

ADDRESS:
A unique identifier for a computer or site online.

AD EXCHANGE:
An open, bid marketplace where premium publishers and ad networks sell their remnant/unsold inventory to advertisers.

AD EXTENSIONS:
Ad extensions are features that may be appended to the end of a search ad, which allow a brand to promote certain information upfront such as an address, phone number, links to other pages of a website, or a special offer.

AD NETWORK:
An aggregator or broker of advertising inventory for many different publishers.

AD RECALL:
A measure of a consumer's likeliness to remember a brand.

AD REQUEST:
The request a browser makes for the ad to be sent from the ad server.

AD SERVER:
A technology platform that allows for the coding, management and tracking of all digital campaigns.

AD SERVING:
The delivery of an ad by a server to a user's computer.

AFFILIATE MARKETING:
A cost-per-action revenue share model between advertisers, publishers and the network.

AFFINITY MARKETING:
Advertising a brand to consumers based on their established buying history.

ANDROID:
Google's mobile operating system.

ANIMATED GIF:
An animation created by combining multiple GIF images in one file.

APP AD EXTENSIONS:
Search ads that have a promotional call-out for a mobile or tablet app, which are appended to the end, underneath the URL.

ATTRIBUTION:
A reporting model that allows marketers to understand a consumer's path to conversion and apply ROI to multiple channels or touch-points.

AUDIENCE TARGETING:
A combination of contextual, demographic, geographic, behavioral and retargeting tactics.

BANNER:
A common form of digital advertising that utilizes a graphic image, or other media object, to promote a brand on a website.

BEHAVIORAL TARGETING:
Following consumers' online habits (clicks, frequency and time spent), a brand's message is delivered when a visitor demonstrates the desired behaviors associated with the brand.

BILLBOARD:
A 970x250 pixel banner.

BRAND AWARENESS:
A measure of how well consumers are able to identify and recall a brand.

BROWSER:
A software program that requests, downloads, caches and displays a webpage.

BLIND AD NETWORK:
An ad network that does not share the list of publishers it works with.

CALL AD EXTENSION:
Search ads that drive consumers to call a brand directly. When served on a desktop or laptop, a phone number is provided, and when served on a mobile device, a click-to-call button is provided.

CHANNEL:
Avenues that are used to make products available.

CLICKS:
A measure of actions taken on a link, whereby a consumer is directed from one page or ad to another.

CLICKTHROUGH RATE:
The ratio of clicks on an ad to the number of impressions served.

COMMUNICATION AD EXTENSION:
Search ads that have a one-step form appended to the end, underneath the URL. They allow consumers to sign up for alerts, updates and offers directly at the ad level, without being directed away from their original search query.

COMPANION AD:
A banner or ad that is shown on the same webpage while a video is playing.

CONNECT RATE:
The ratio of visits to a landing page versus clicks on a banner.

CONTAINER TAG:
A snippet of web code added to a webpage, which enables actions such as visits, conversions and purchase information to be recorded. It also contains functionality to piggyback other snippets of web code.

CONTENT INTEGRATION:
Advertising woven into a publisher's editorial content

CONTENT SYNDICATION:
A method where a brand's assets (whitepapers, webinars or videos) are dispersed through a network of websites. To access the brand's assets, prospective consumers complete a gated registration form. The registration data is then sent to the brand as a lead.

CONTEXTUAL TARGETING:
Delivers the brand message on webpages containing content that is specified by the advertiser as relevant or desirable.

CONVERSIONS:
The number of consumers that responded to a campaign's call to action. Conversions are typically form completes or other high value engagements.

CONVERSION RATE:
The ratio of conversions recorded versus visits to the landing page.

COOKIE:
A small program code that is stored on a browser to track web history, saved passwords and links.

COST-PER-ACTION (CPA):
The cost for each recorded action. An action may be a lead, sale, conversion, or any other metric agreed upon.

COST-PER-CLICK (CPC):
The cost for each recorded click.

COST-PER-CONVERSION:
The cost for each conversion recorded.

COST-PER-SALE:
The cost for each recorded sale.

COST-PER-THOUSAND IMPRESSIONS (CPM):
The price to purchase 1,000 impressions. It is the standard pricing model used across media channels.

DEDICATED EMAIL:
A custom email that is sent to a publisher's list of subscribers on behalf of a brand.

DEDUPLICATED AUDIENCE:
The number of unique individuals that visit a webpage, or see a brand's message, within a specified timeframe.

DEMAND SIDE PLATFORM (DSP):
A technology platform that automatically reads, scores then bids on impressions in real time for an advertiser within the exchanges.

DEMOGRAPHICS:
Quantifiable statistics of a given population, such as age, gender and household income.

DEMOGRAPHIC TARGETING:
Using registration data, survey data or third party data, an ad is delivered to target individuals based on their demographic profiles. Some common demographic data include gender, age, and education level.

DISPLAY:
A common form of digital advertising that utilizes a graphic image, or other media object, to promote a brand on a website. Banner advertising is now referred to as display.

EXPANDABLE BANNER:
Banners, that when click upon or hovered over by a mouse, expand to a larger size.

FIXED RATE:
A hard cost set by a vendor, often used for sponsorships, content syndication, and other premium media placements.

FLASH BANNERS:
Banners that are created with Adobe Flash.

FLOATING ADS:
Banners that appear over the content of a webpage.

FOLLOWER:
Twitter users who subscribe to another Twitter account.

FREQUENCY:
The number of times an ad is delivered to a unique browser, and hopefully a consumer, within a given timeframe.

FREQUENCY CAP:
Restrictions placed on the number of times an ad is delivered to a unique browser, and hopefully, a consumer.

FULL BANNER:
A 468x60 pixel banner.

GEO-TARGETING:
An ad targeted based on a user's specific location

GRAPHIC INTERCHANGE FORMAT (GIF):
Any combination of static or animated

imagery created in a .gif format.

HALF PAGE BANNER:
A 300x600 pixel banner.

HOME PAGE:
The page designated as the main point of entry to a website.

HOST:
Also known as a server, a host is a computer which distributes files that are shared across a LAN, WAN or the Internet.

IAB RISING STARS:
A collection of newly popular media placements, recognized by the IAB, that have been given standardized specifications for media vendors to follow.

INTERACTIVE ADVERTISING BUREAU (IAB):
A non-profit digital advertising trade association. See iab.net for more details.

IMPRESSION:
The number of times a brand's ad is served on a webpage.

IN-BANNER VIDEOS:
Videos that play within a standard banner.

INFERRED DATA:
Data gleaned from click, cookie, survey or other inferred information.

INSERTION ORDER:
A legally binding sales agreement between a brand and a media vendor for the purchase of media space.

IN-STREAM:
Ads that are auto-played within publishers' digital video content.

INTERSTITIAL ADS:
Ads that serve before a webpage loads.

IOS:
Apple's mobile operating system.

IP ADDRESS:
An internet protocol numerical address that is assigned to each computer in order to track its usage and location.

KEY PERFORMANCE INDICATORS:
The metrics used to gauge a digital campaign's success.

LARGE RECTANGLE:
A 336x280 pixel banner.

LEAD:
Identifying data (name, address, email, phone number) captured by an advertising program. Leads represent prospective customers.

LEADERBOARD:
A 728x90 pixel banner.

LEAD GENERATION:
The generation of consumer inquiry requests for a specific product or asset.

LIKE:
A method of feedback created by Facebook for users to show their affinity for a page, comment, photo or other content across the web.

LOCAL AD NETWORK:
An aggregator and broker of regional websites.

LOCATION AD EXTENSION:
Search ads that have an address and phone number appended to the end, underneath the URL. They are typically used to drive consumers offline and into a nearby store.

LOOK-ALIKE MODELING:
Finds consumers that display similar behavioral patterns across the Internet as those that have converted for the brand already.

LONG TAIL AD NETWORK:
An ad network focused on aggregating

and brokering content from comScore's extended list of media properties – sites that are much smaller and less known across the Internet.

MEDIUM RECTANGLE:
A 300x250 pixel banner.

MICROSITES:
A subpage of a wepage, that stands alone from the rest of the website.

MID-ROLL:
An ad that is delivered mid-stream of an online video, similar to a TV commercial break.

MOBILE ADVERTISING:
Advertising displayed on a mobile device.

NEWS FEED:
A list of real-time updates on a user's Facebook homepage from friends and pages followed.

NEWSLETTER SPONSORSHIP:
An ad placement within a publisher's newsletter that is sent out to its subscribers. Ad placement include banner ads and text ads.

OFFER AD EXTENSION:
Search ads that have a discount offer or coupon appended to the end, underneath the URL.

OVERLAYS:
Banners that appear over the content of a webpage.

PAGE VIEW:
A measure that counts when a webpage is fully loaded.

PEELBACKS:
Rich media ads that when clicked upon or rolled over, unveil themselves across the content of a page, as if the click was turning a page in a book.

PENCIL:
Also known as a portrait ad, is a 970x90 pixel banner.

PIXEL:
A single picture element (1x1 units) used for image display. It is also enables third party tracking code.

POP-UPS:
Ad units that open in a new web browser window, in front of the window being viewed.

POP-UNDERS:
Ad units that open in a new web browser window, behind the window being viewed.

POST-ROLL:
An ad that is delivered after viewing an online video.

PORTRAIT:
Also known as a pencil ad, is a 970x90 pixel banner.

PREMIUM AD NETWORK:
An ad network focused on aggregating and brokering content from comScore's list of the top 100 media properties – most trafficked and well known sites across the Internet.

PRE-ROLL:
An ad is delivered prior to the streaming of an online video.

PRODUCT LISTING ADS (PLAS):
The search ads that have featured products appended to the end, underneath the URL. They are used to highlight products that are already listed under a brand's Google Merchant Center (GMC) account.

PROFILING:
The tracking of consumers' demographic and psychographic information in order to build a profile of that consumer.

PUBLISHER:
An individual or organization that prepares, issues, and disseminates content for public distribution or sale via one or more media.

PUSHDOWN:
An expandable banner located at the top of a webpage that expands downward, over the content of the page, when rolled over or clicked.

RAILS:
Skyscraper style ads that line both the right and left side of a webpage.

RATE CARD:
An outline of a media vendor's placements, products and their associated costs.

REACH:
The count of unique users that have visited a webpage within a given timeframe, or a percentage of an audience.

REAL-TIME:
Data that is tracked and delivered immediately, without any delays.

REAL-TIME BIDDING (RTB):
Bids for impressions or clicks that happen immediately, without any delays.

RE-DIRECT:
A URL or a page that instantly and automatically directs a user to another page.

RECTANGLE:
A 180x150 pixel banner.

REFERRAL URL:
The webpage that a user was visiting prior to reaching their current page.

REGISTRATION DATA:
User defined information that is voluntarily given to a website.

REPEAT VISITOR:
A unique visitor that has gone to a website two or more times during a specified timeframe.

RETARGETING:
Sometimes referred to as remarketing, retargeting re-delivers the brand's message to consumers that have already been exposed to the brand— seen an ad, visited the brand's website, or engaged.

RETURN ON INVESTMENT (ROI):
The ratio of net profit versus investment.

RETURN VISITS:
The average number of times a unique user returns to a website within a specific timeframe.

RICH MEDIA:
Banners that are advanced coded to do one or more of the following things: expand, play a video, house a survey, feed in content, be re-posted, house a game, dynamically adapt, capture data, animate and more.

ROADBLOCK:
A premium 100% share-of-voice

takeover of all banners on a webpage.

RUN OF NETWORK:
No defined targeting restrictions, reaches everyone across an ad network.

RUN OF SITE:
No defined targeting restrictions, reaches everyone across a website.

RSS/ RSS READERS:
Really Simple Syndication – a process for publishing content on the Internet by transferring it from one location to another.

SEARCH ADS:
Text ads that commonly appear within Google, Bing or Yahoo search results. They are used to place a brand's message at the critical moment when a comsumer is actively looking for a particular brand or solution via keyword search.

SEARCH ENGINE MARKETING (SEM):
A form of internet marketing, where marketers pay to promote and rank ads or webpages within search engines like Google or Bing.

SEARCH ENGINE OPTIMIZATION (SEO):
Non-paid strategies and tactical approaches used to increase a website's rank within search engines like Google or Bing.

SELLER AD EXTENSION:
Search ads that have consumer review ratings appended directly after the title, above the body copy.

SERVER:
Also known as a host, a server is a computer which distributes files that are shared across a LAN, WAN or the Internet.

SHARE OF VOICE:
The percentage of ad impressions a brand receives compared to others.

SIDEKICK:
A 300x250 pixel banner that expands into an 850x700 pixel banner when clicked upon or rolled over.

SITELINKS AD EXTENSION:
Search ads that have up to four URLs appended to the end.

SKINS:
Customizable and interchangeable background graphics for a browser, webpage or desktop.

SKYSCRAPER:
A 160x600 pixel banner. May also be a 120x600 pixel banner.

SLIDER:
A 90x500 pixel banner that expands into a 950x550 pixel banner when clicked upon or rolled over.

SMALL RECTANGLE:
A 180x150 pixel banner.

SMARTPHONE:
A handheld device that integrates mobile calling with internet capabilities such as email, applications, and other tasks previously attributed to desktop devices.

SOCIAL AD EXTENSION:
Search ads that have the number of people that have followed the brand or +1'd in Google+ appended to the end, underneath the URL.

SOCIAL TARGETING:
Ads are delivered to individuals, or like individuals, based on their digital social connections and profiles.

SPIDER:
A program, often called a bot (short for robot), that automatically crawls across the web reading and gathering content for websites and search engines.

SPONSORSHIP:
Custom content and/or experiences on a webpage, which are specifically created for a brand's promotional message.

SPONSOR:
A relationship between a brand and a publisher, by which a specific portion of a website is co-promoted.

STANDARD BANNER:
Any combination of static or animated imagery and text that are housed within a .jpg or .gif file.

TABLET:
A mobile device used to browse the web, access email, run applications, and other computing tasks.

TARGET AUDIENCE:
The intended audience for a brand's ad, typically defined by a combination of demographic and/or psychographic information.

TEXT ADS:
Text only ads, that usually have a title, body copy and clickthrough URL.

TEXTLINKS:
Single-line text ads, or simple text on a webpage.

THROUGHPUT:
The number of data requests handled within a given timeframe. Throughput is used to measure a website's server performance.

TIMELINE:
Facebook's personal profile page or Twitter's real-time news feed of tweets.

TIME SPENT:
The amount of time a visitor spends on a webpage.

TRADING DESK:
An agency's or holding company's department for dealing with DSPs. These agencies and holding companies partner with a DSP to license their algorithm to purchase

inventory from the exchanges.

TRAFFIC:
The flow of visitors to a website.

TRANSPARENT:
Ad networks that share the fill list of publishers they work with.

TWEET:
140-character messages, published on the Twitter platform.

UNIQUE USER/VISITOR:
A unique individual that has visited a webpage, or accessed content such as a brand's ad or email.

USER REGISTRATION:
User defined information, voluntarily given to a website.

VERTICAL NETWORK:
An ad network of websites that fall under a single content category.

VIEW:
The number of times a brand's ad is seen.

VIEW THROUGH:
A metric used in Display to measure the number of indirect visits or actions that occur as a result of an ad being viewed, but not clicked.

VIRAL MARKETING:
Any advertising that is picked up and passed along from one consumer to another via email, social sharing or word of mouth.

VIRAL VIDEO:
Online video clips that are picked up and passed along from one consumer to another.

VIRTUAL CONFERENCE:
Virtual presentations, which usually include real-time question and answer sessions afterwards.

VISIT:
The total number of times a browser views a webpage.

WEBINAR:
A web-based seminar in the format of a multimedia presentation, workshop, or lecture, that allows for interaction between the presenter and audience.

WEBSITE:
The virtual location of an individual or organization's content on the Internet.

WHITEPAPER:
An authoritative report, guide or analysis used by companies to promote a topic, product or message.

WHITEPAPER LIBRARY:
A searchable collection of whitepapers that are grouped by content and often

gated by a registration form.

WHITEPAPER SYNDICATION:
The dissemination and promotion
of whitepapers.

YIELD:
The ratio of a conversion metric (click
or other action taken) versus the
volume of impressions delivered.